Contents

Dirt Diggers — page 4

How They Work — page 8

Buckets and Blades — page 13

Dirty Jobs — page 20

Backhoe Diagram — page 28

Fun Facts — page 29

Glossary — page 30

Further Reading — page 31

Index — page 32

Dirt Diggers

Do you like to dig in the dirt?

Earthmovers dig tons of dirt.
They dig sand too. Dirt and sand
are kinds of earth. Earthmovers
are made to move earth.

They push earth.
They scoop earth.

This earthmover scoops and dumps out a large pile of earth.

They pack it down hard.

How They Work

An operator makes an earthmover go. An earthmover's operator sits in the cab.

An engine gives an earthmover power.

An earthmover's engine is underneath or behind the cab.

The engine makes an earthmover's tracks go around. Tracks keep an earthmover from sinking in soft dirt.

Dirt covers this earthmover's tracks.

Some earthmovers have rubber tires, not tracks. But tires can sink in soft dirt. They work best on hard dirt and roads.

An earthmover's engine makes its arm go up and down too. What is at the end of this earthmover's arm? A bucket is at the end of the arm.

Buckets and Blades

Front-end loaders have wide buckets. They are good for scooping earth.

This front-end loader has a full bucket.

Skid-steer loaders have buckets with flat bottoms. They can scoop or push earth.

Do you see the flat bottom on this skid-steer loader's bucket?

Excavators have big buckets called hoes. They can dig and dump piles of dirt.

Backhoes have two buckets.
The wide one in front is good
for scooping.

A backhoe can scoop
a lot of dirt with its
front bucket.

The bucket in back is a hoe. That is why these earthmovers are called backhoes.

The backhoe digs holes with its back bucket.

Some earthmovers have flat blades instead of buckets. **Bulldozers have blades. They push big piles of earth.**

This is the blade of a bulldozer.

Graders have blades too. The blade is behind the front tires. It makes the earth smooth, like frosting on a cake.

Dirty Jobs

Each earthmover has a job to do. Look at the bucket. Look at the tracks. Can you guess what job this earthmover is doing?

This excavator is digging a hole for a new building. The operator dumps earth in a truck. The truck driver takes it away.

This earthmover has a
funny shape.

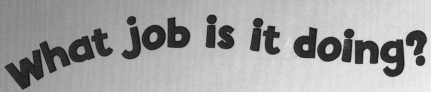

What job is it doing?

This scraper is working on a
new road. A wide pan hangs
down in the middle of the
scraper. Dirt slides into the
pan as the scraper rolls along.

After the scraper, along comes
a grader. Graders roll quickly
on rubber tires. They make
the dirt smooth and flat.

Next come rollers to pack the dirt. This sheepsfoot roller has bumps. The bumps leave a pattern in the dirt.

If you see a pattern like this in the dirt, you'll know a sheepsfoot roller has been by.

Earthmovers move earth.
They dig in the dirt all day.

These earthmovers line up and shut down after a long day's work.

The earthmovers' work is done for the day.

Backhoe Diagram

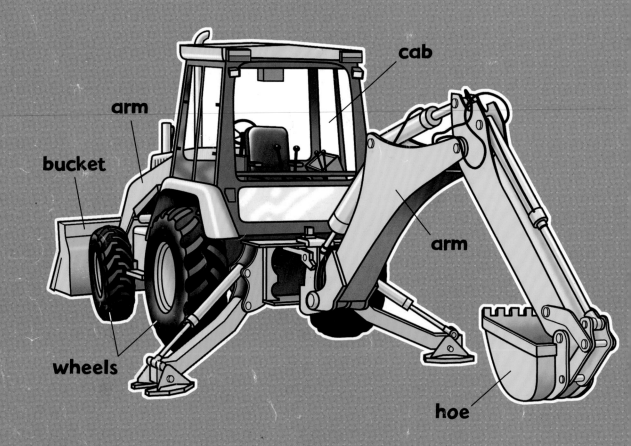

cab

arm

bucket

arm

wheels

hoe

Fun Facts

- Excavators have different nicknames in different parts of the United States. In some places, they are called shovels. In other places, they are called hoes.

- When is a bobcat not a real cat? When it's a skid-steer loader. Skid-steer loaders are often called bobcats. A company called Bobcat makes many skid-steer loaders.

- A large excavator can fill a whole dump truck with dirt from just two scoops of its bucket.

- The sheepsfoot roller got its name from the prints it makes in the earth. It makes the ground look like hundreds of sheep walked over it.

Glossary

arm: the part of an earthmover that connects the main part to another part that digs or scoops

blade: the wide, flat part of a bulldozer or grader that pushes or smooths earth

bucket: the part of an earthmover that scoops and digs earth

engine: the part of an earthmover that gives it power and makes its parts move

hoe: a special kind of bucket on an excavator or a backhoe that digs earth

operator: the person who makes an earthmover work

tracks: wide belts that carry earthmovers over soft dirt

Further Reading

Brecke, Nicole, and Patricia M. Stockland.
Cars, Trucks, and Motorcycles You Can Draw.
Minneapolis: Millbrook Press, 2010.

Enchanted Learning: Vehicle Online Coloring Pages
http://www.enchantedlearning.com/vehicles/
paintonline.shtml

Harris, Nicholas. *A Year at a Construction Site.*
Minneapolis: Millbrook Press, 2009.

Martin, M. T. *Earth Movers.* Minneapolis:
Bellwether Media, 2007.

Tieck, Sarah. *Earth Movers.* Edina, MN: Abdo,
2005.

Index

arm, 12, 28

blades, 18–19
bucket, 12–18, 20, 28–29

engine, 9–10, 12

hoes, 15, 17, 28–29

kinds of earthmovers, 13–19, 23, 25

operator, 8, 21

tires, 11, 19, 24
tracks, 10–11, 20

Photo Acknowledgments

The images in this book are used with the permission of: © Yegorius/Shutterstock Images, p. 1; Courtesy John Deere & Company, pp. 2, 5, 13, 16, 17; © Kitti/Shutterstock Images, p. 4; © Construction Photography/CORBIS, p. 6; © Bobbie66/Shutterstock Images, p. 7; © Jim Zuckerman/Alamy, p. 8; © fine art/Alamy, p. 9; © Ed Darack/Science Faction/CORBIS, p. 10; © Titelio/Dreamstime.com, p. 11; © Heinrich van den Berg/Gallo Images/Getty Images, p. 12; © Gualberto Becerra/Shutterstock Images, p. 14; © aba ssaka/Shutterstock Images, p. 15; © Stephen McSweeny/Shutterstock Images, p. 18; © Gorben/Shutterstock Images, p. 19; © Mishoo/Dreamstime.com, p. 20; © StockImages/Alamy, p. 21; © Jim Parkin/Alamy, p. 22; © Bill Marsh Royalty Free Photography/Alamy, p. 23; © Holly Pickett/Spokane Spokesman-Review/WpN/Photoshot, p. 24; © PhotoSpin, Inc./Alamy, p. 25; © Mark Segal/Stone/Getty Images, p. 26; © Patrick Clark/Photodisc/Getty Images, p. 27; © Laura Westlund/Independent Picture Service, p. 28; © bhathaway/Shutterstock Images, p. 29; © Matt Richard/iStockphoto.com, p. 30; © Marksim Toome/Shutterstock Images, p. 31.

Front cover: Courtesy John Deere & Company (excavator); © Photodisc/Getty Images (bucket loader).

In memory of my
dear friend Izzy
—L.S.H.

Lerner Publications Company
A division of Lerner Publishing Group, Inc.
241 First Avenue North
Minneapolis, MN 55401 U.S.A.

Website address: www.lernerbooks.com

Library of Congress Cataloging-in-Publication Data

Hill, Lee Sullivan, 1958–
    Earthmovers on the move / by Lee Sullivan Hill.
        p.   cm. — (Lightning bolt books™ — Vroom-vroom)
    Includes index.
    ISBN 978–0–7613–3918–2 (lib. bdg. : alk. paper)
    1. Earthmoving machinery—Juvenile literature. I. Title.
    TA725.H54 2011
    621.8'65—dc22   2009039739

Manufactured in the United States of America
1 — BP — 7/15/10

LIGHT BOOKS™

Earthmovers
on the Move

Lee Sullivan Hill

Lerner Publications Company

Minneapolis